Ants: The True Story

by Robert Bridges
illustrated by John Hovell

Core Decodable 92

McGraw Hill Education

Bothell, WA • Chicago, IL • Columbus, OH • New York, NY

MHEonline.com

Send all inquiries to:
McGraw-Hill Education
8787 Orion Place
Columbus, OH 43240

ISBN: 978-0-02-144904-0
MHID: 0-02-144904-X

Printed in China

7 8 9 10 11 DSS 27 26 25 24 23

Ants fool humans.

Humans think we just dig nests.

They think we dig like bugs.

But that is not the truth.
We use tools to dig.
We use drills and spades.

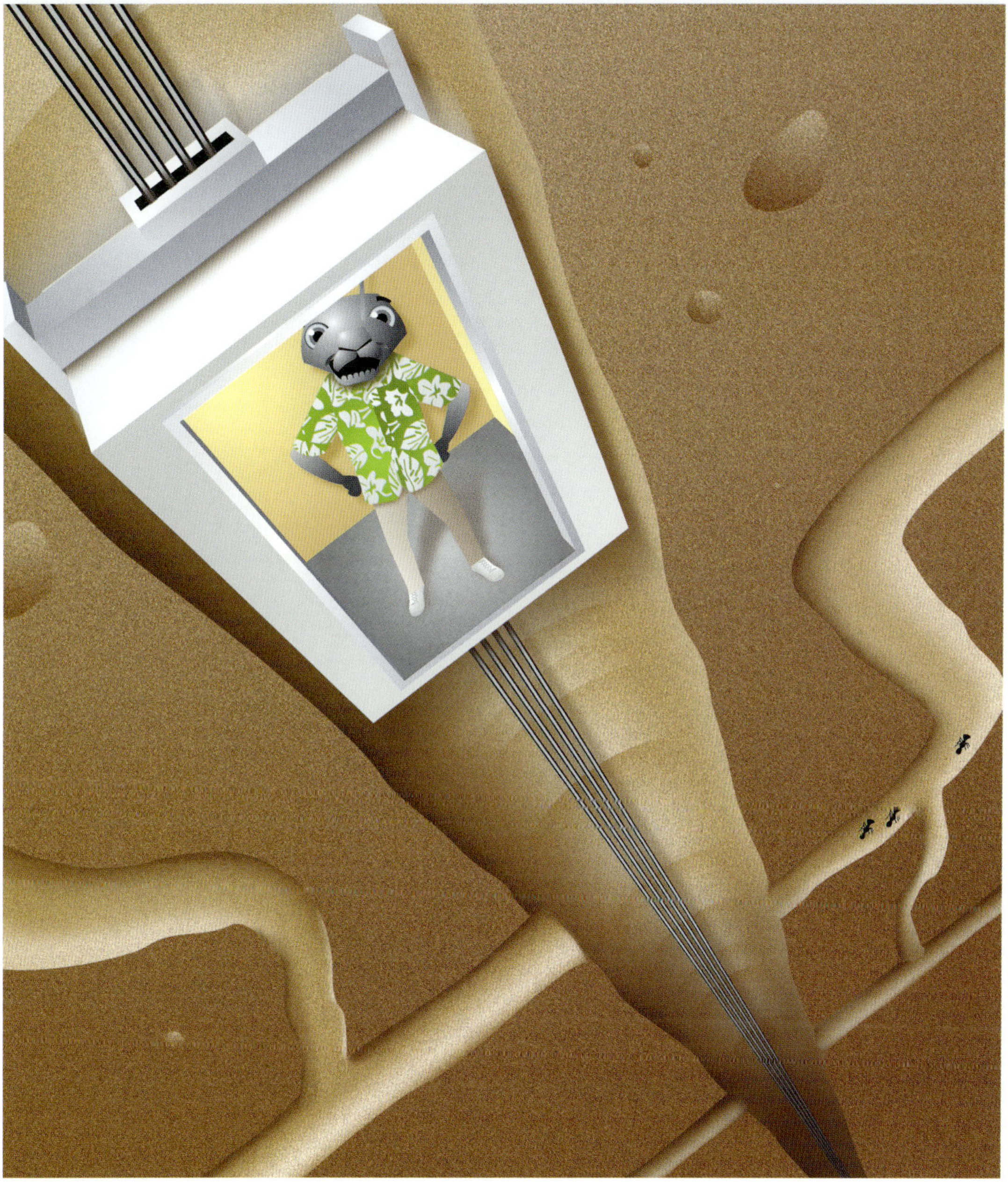

And ants do not walk down.
We zoom down in nests.
It is a fast, smooth ride.

Down below we have rooms.
The rooms have walls.
My room is painted blue.

Humans think we store food.
Well, we truly do.
But not the way humans think.

This room is for food.
We keep this room cool.
Then food stays fresh.

What do ants eat?
Humans do not have a clue!
Ants eat the best food.

Do ants like sweets?

We do, but we eat healthy food, too.

After we eat, we clean up.
Ants must do their duty.
I use a broom.

In the evening, ants rest.
Some hear music.
Two ants play a tuba duet.

Some ants read.

Some read papers.

I am reading a story.

Ants get exercise, too.
We swim in a pool under a glass roof.
Some ants dance in tutus.

I can float on my back.
I can see the moon.

So this is the real story.

It is all true.

Ants fool humans.